Common Sense in 21st Century

By Tony Butler

Table of Contents

Preface

This book although political in context, is written in a matter to make it more appealing and accessible to everyone with a third grade reading level.

Like in the third grade we start learning about our country, its founding and the struggles of the colonist to gain their independence.

We the people have reached a point in time where we have another struggle on our hands, to gain our independence once again. Not from a dictating king in a foreign land but a dictating federal government that infringes on our every move as a free people.

Introduction

Nearly two hundred and fifty years ago a patriot named Thomas Paine wrote a short book called Common Sense. From these writings, an American Revolution was born, as nearly every colonist had read it or had it read to them.

Here we are nearly two hundred and fifty years later and in desperate need for a new infusion of common sense as it pertains to our federal government.

A new American Revolution is much needed, in a bloodless fashion of course, not to replace the government our founding fathers created, but to restore it to its original intent and ideals of the constitution.

We do need a strong central federal government from a military and a security perspective. But do we really need the federal government to dictate our every move from what our children eat at school to deliver the mail.

Most Americans are unaware of just how much intrusion into their daily lives the federal government participates.

The intention of this book is to try and instill some common sense ideas and approaches to a wide array of topics that do concern or quietly affect every American to a certain extent.

The most disturbing thing about our politicians and every American today as well, is their unbelievable stubbornness to accept the fact that someone might have a different thought or opinion on a subject other than their own.

In the last fifteen years it seems our politicians would prefer absolute total gridlock over compromise. Our presidents have used more executive orders to circumvent the Congress or the law than ever before.

The first 200 years or so our political system worked pretty well no matter which party was in control of the White House or Congress. Those party leaders were willing to compromise. Each side was willing to give and take and the system worked fairly well.

Somehow in the last fifteen years it seems like all Americans and our politicians are not only not willing to compromise on anything but they have totally forgotten about how this country was founded and what it is suppose to stand for in the first place.

Freedom of religion was the foundation for which this nation was founded and now it seems for some reason that some people are offended by the sight of a cross.

This sudden rush- of people to be offended by the simplest things and others to quickly comment on the side of political correctness is approaching absolute absurdity.

We as a people need to step back, take a deep breathe, and just think for a minute. Think about the hundreds of thousands of your forefathers who gave the ultimate sacrifice so we can have the basic freedoms of religion, speech, and thought.

Think how wrong it is for you to be upset with someone just because they don't agree with you on a particular subject. Think how a closed mind is a terrible waste. Without open-minded people nothing would ever get invented, created, and perhaps even written.

This author does not wish fame or fortune or have any political ambition nor a political agenda. It is very popular today for people to attack the messenger instead of the message.

There will be some things you will agree with and some you will disagree with. If there's something you disagree with. spend your time thinking of an alternative idea or solution. Social change begins with a single thought.

At a later date hopefully there will be a website created where ideas, thoughts, and discussions can be made on wide array of subjects.

If one idea from this book results in some sort of

positive social change, then the whole thing would have been worth the time and effort.

Common Sense Campaign Reform

Nothing can be changed in Washington D.C. or your state houses until real campaign finance is changed. Until you take the power of the all mighty dollar out of the equation nothing is going to change in government. The lobbyists and special interest groups are always going to have real control of our government as long as their money dictates everything that happens or doesn't happen.

We can't make any real positive changes in state or federal government until we have some common sense approach to funding political campaigns.

The sensible thing to do is use tax dollars to fund all campaigns. This would instantly restore the power to, We the People, and take it away from the lobbyist and special interest groups.

Just imagine the reduction in the size of government spending if you took out all the corporate welfare and spending on special interest groups.

On the other side of the coin is the increase in tax revenues that would result. Both parties are guilty of attaching amendments to bills providing tax breaks for corporations, typically in exchange for campaign contributions.

That is why the politicians all say they are for real tax reform but seriously can't do anything about it.

Every fiscal year there should be so much money allocated to an escrow account for each senate and congressional seat on an equal basis for each party, the Democrats and the Republicans and in the same way for the presidential campaigns. Finally a sensible campaign finance reform would be in place that would obligate the politicians to the people as it should have been, not the lobbyists or special interest groups that buy their political support.

Common Sense Legislative Reform

For years there has been lots of discussion about term limits for both congressmen and even governors at the state level. Term limits should be decided on by the voters. What is truly needed is legislative limits.

After two hundred and fifty years of thousands of pages of new laws, year after year, term limits for our politicians isn't the problem, excessive legislature is.

When they passed the Affordable Care Act they hurried around and voted on it before anyone had a chance to read it. Stop the insanity!

The only way to sensibly control Congress is to put legislative limits on them. They should be restricted to only submit one piece of legislation each per year. That would still be 535 pieces of legislation each year from the House and Senate. At least if it is done this way they'd be able to read what they are voting on.

This would only work if the limits included

amendments as well. Otherwise they'd submit one bill each and them turn around and attach a hundred amendments.

Imagine if you will, a Congress that doesn't have to spend all their time raising money or courting lobbyists and special interest groups over thousands of pages of new legislation every year. Think of the time they'd have on their hands to actually think about how to better serve the people.

That time would be better spent to evaluate our government agencies, to eliminate duplication of services, to provide better government instead of simply more of it.

Think of the possibilities; an actual energy policy, real healthcare reform, rebuild our nation's infrastructure. Things people really care about with an effect on their daily lives.

Common Sense Tax Reform

The only sensible way to real tax reform is start by totally scrapping our current system.

The whole complicated system of thousands of pages of tax laws and deductions furthermore filing all of the tax returns by April 15 is totally insane. Let's just scrap the whole system and simplify it.

The average working man or woman that draws a weekly paycheck for a living should never have to file their income taxes at all. Their employer simply deducts their taxes just like they do today and their taxes are paid. End of story.

This insanity of tax forms and deductions and filing and some paying in but most receiving refunds is ridiculous.

All businesses, from the smallest to the largest corporations, would pay an easy to compute gross revenue tax. Since the goal of every businessman in the country today is to increase sales or revenue, the flat tax on gross revenue would be an easy to calculate therefore easy to determine the price of their goods and services. Businesses would still pay on a quarterly basis, just like they do today.

The capital gains tax should be for the most part eliminated. After all, most wealth created in this country was taxed to begin with and to tax it again after it is invested in economic and job creating enterprises seems to undermine the concept of capitalism.

However, the huge stock options that the corporations give their executives should be taxed at regular income tax rates. If they want to overpay their executives, the corporation should buy the stock on the open-market, give it to the executive who in turn would have to sell at least half of it to pay the taxes. At least this way the shareholders wouldn't have to foot the bill for the deletion of stockholders equity every time they issue stock options for the executives.

A common sense approach to tax code always

faces the toughest fight. There are thousands of people, lawyers, accountants and tax preparers not to mention all of the government employees that thrive on the complications of our tax code. So making changes as drastic as this would have the toughest uphill battle.

Common Sense Government Regulation

There is no doubt there is a need for government regulation. Human nature dictates it. Otherwise people would sell or do almost anything for money if there was no oversight by someone. The single largest problem with government regulation is the fact that those that pass or impose the regulation know almost nothing or very little about the businesses in which they are regulating. On the other hand you can't have the businesses regulate themselves for obvious reasons.

The sensible approach would be if each regulating commission would have a three-sided board of members, then an equal amount of representatives from each business in need of regulating should be selected. There should be an equal number of regulators and an equal number of bipartisan academia members.

The neutral academia members would act more as a referee between business and government, insure or try to insure against corruption if possible and act as a compromiser between government and business.

Much of the government spending and regulation should be left up to each individual state. The federal funding should be issued to each state in the form of block grants and let each state spend the money according to how they see fit.

Most regulation should be managed by each state not the federal government. This country is comprised of 320 million human beings. Humans are not in any way perfect. They are going to do stupid things. It's human nature. Every time someone does something stupid there's a rush to think we need a whole new set of regulations or laws to prevent this stupidity from happening again.

In most cases there are already laws in place that have been violated. It seems the politicians like the publicity and like to show their voters that they care and are doing something about it.

Common Sense Healthcare Reform

Approximately half the costs of healthcare are associated with the sales and marketing of insurance and the billing and administration for healthcare services by the providers. In other words, about half the cost of healthcare has nothing to do with the actual healthcare in itself, but with the bureaucracy that has been created in the last fifty years.

If you could drastically reduce the amount of this paper work you could save everyone billions of dollars. A sensible approach would be to treat healthcare like a utility, like your light company, cable television or sewer and water.

Your healthcare provider would have a franchise authority just like any other utility. Monthly billing should be calculated by taking the number of members per household. No sales commission marketing costs or billing over every little service provided would be necessary.

As far as Medicaid and the low income people are concerned the government would simply cut the healthcare provider a check each month based on the number of people in the programs in their coverage area.

Imagine the cost savings if all doctors were salaried instead of a high fee based compensation. Of course, to accommodate anyone that wants to enter the medical field at every level from nurses aids to doctors in specialized fields. Incentives should be given to assist in student loans and also put them in low or no income tax brackets. Make it financially rewarding to still enter the medical profession but in a way that reduces the cost of healthcare for everyone.

Common Sense Welfare Reform

Now it has currently been reported that there are some 11 million people receiving some form of disability checks. There is no doubt that there are disabled people that need assistance but on the other hand there are countless others who are taking advantage of the system when they are perfectly capable of doing some kind of work.

Workfare instead of welfare makes more sense for everyone involved. There are millions of low paying minimum wage jobs that employers have a difficult time filling and maintaining. By using workfare, the employer would pay the minimum wage and workfare would subsidize the rest. If your goal for example was $15 an hour, minimum wage and the state minimum wage was say $7, the employer would pay $7 and workfare would pay the remaining $8 per hour.

Minimum hours of say 20 per week would help the employers maintain a somewhat stable workforce.

You could expand this program for students by using their workfare subsidy to pay down on their student loans. Anyway you look at it, more would benefit from a workfare type program, from the employers to the government in an actual reduction in cost of the current welfare state. Of course, the truly disabled would receive an exemption from participating in such a program.

The way the Aid to Dependent Children program is currently operating there is absolutely no incentive whatsoever to ever get off of such a program once you began. In fact the more children you have, the more money you get.

There should be a program for young mothers to allow them to further their education, work part time, and still receive ADC. The added the cost of such a program would be offset by future savings as these women would hopefully be off the ADC program entirely someday.

Common Sense Social Security

There has been some discussion about a needs testing to receive Social Security benefits, in other words, the wealthiest of Americans wouldn't receive their Social Security benefits upon retirement.

The simplest way to do this would be to raise the overall tax rate on the wealthiest of people that receive Social Security and lower overall rate for those same wealthy individuals that don't, thereby giving the wealthy an incentive to decline receiving their Social Security checks in the first place.

The savings of not including the wealthiest people in receiving Social Security benefits can be used to increase the benefits for the poorest of Americans.

There have been various plans proposed on how to fix Social Security. Most have something to do with a privatization and voluntary savings plan but most of these that propose such a plan don't take into count the reason Social Security was formed in the first place. Any type of plan must be made mandatory for all those to participate in, otherwise, too many wouldn't and the majority of those that would are the wealthiest of Americans who don't need it in the first place.

Common Sense Immigration

Most of the immigration concerns we have today are in regard to our southern border. Did anyone ever think about simply taking bulldozers and pushing the cactus and mesquite trees into piles along the border for a barrier? Just imagine a ten feet high thicket of cactus and mesquite, nobody would try to climb over the top of that stuff. It would be the least expensive wall you could build.

There should be a system in place for workers from south of the border to get work visas. Many industries need the help and have difficult time in filling these positions.

The real problem is the drug cartels and the Mexican government. Soon as we get our own economy going again our first objective should be to help get the Mexican economy going as soon as the drug cartels have been squashed.

Common Sense Legal System

It's embarrassing as a nation to have almost two million people in our prison system. Not to mention the cost of billions of dollars. Then there is the wasted lives of many who end up spending most of their adult lives in prison not only because of poor judgment but because of total loss of hope and despair.

The whole insanity of a judge sentencing someone to ten years in prisoned, then having them get paroled in three years plus all of the bureaucracy involved with parole officers and so on, is both very costly and nonproductive.

First, in order to help cut the costs of our legal system all lawyers, in order to maintain their law practice and license should be required to provide a certain number of hours in a public defender service. The number of hours could be calculated by the number of hours needed, divided by the total number of lawyers practicing in the state. This would save each state millions of dollars.

Secondly, as soon as an individual enters the prison system he should be given a test to evaluate their level of reading, writing, and arithmetic and general aptitude. Everyone within the system should be required to obtain their GED or high school diploma.

The general aptitude test should be given to see what area each individual could possibly succeed in after rehabilitIf were going to spend a ridiculous amount of money to incarcerate these people, we should just as well form our prison system into a giant trade school. There is always going to be a need of a countless number of tradesman ranging from heavy equipment operators to carpenters, mechanics and plumbers. Give the ex-con a trade of any kind and give hope, a chance, an opportunity to make a good honest living instead of a life of hopeless, depression and despair. Do this and make taxpayers out of them instead of a lifetime where they are in and out and clogging up our legal system.

Of course the success of this program couldn't possibly begin without first helping those that need it with drug and alcohol rehabilitation.

Another thing that needs to be looked into is the mandatory sentencing that forces judges to send people to life in prison for what could be three nonviolent petty crimes.

A review of all these cases on an individual basis should be done at once and those having served long sentences for three petty crimes should be released at once, both as a matter of fairness and a matter of practicality. We are spending way too much money to imprison these people unjustly.

As far as all the violent murderers that are going to live in prison for life, there has got to be a way to make a productive use out of them.

For example, let them choose life or death. If they choose death and agree to donate their organs, everything from the heart to eyes, kidneys, liver, or blood, the state would agree to give their family a financial reward of some kind. Why not help their family out financially instead of wasting their life away in prison. The savings from years of imprisonment could be used to subsidize this program. Also there is the benefit for those that would receive their organs as well.

Another thing all prisoners should have the opportunity to donate blood, especially those with rare and hard to find types.

Special privileges could be extended to those that would participate.

Another possibility for all the lifers is for them to act as human guinea pigs so to speak for drug companies in testing new drugs to help speed up the process for drug companies to get new drugs on the market and FDA approval. There again the drug companies could financially reward the participants families or them personally.

As far as grade and high school funding is concerned the federal funding should provide lump sum funding directly to the state.

Leave it to local and state government to run their schools as they see fit. We don't need federal rules and mandates to run our schools from Washington D.C.

It would also be nice if the teacher unions had just a fraction of concern for the students as they do supporting the teachers that do an inadequate job.

In order to improve education in the poorer communities those teachers and administrators that work in these areas should be given special incentives such as low or no federal tax rates and student loan forgiveness plans. Special tax waivers would save everyone involved, federal, state governments and improve the schools as well.

If every parent of college bound student in this

country knew about the massive endowments our major universities have, there probably be an uprising like you cannot imagine.

For example, Harvard University alone has over a $30 billion endowment. There are over one hundred and fifty universities with $1 billion or more endowments. A total of two hundred and fifty universities have endowments greater than $500 million.

The government spends about $60 billion a year on upper education. That means the top two hundred and fifty universities alone could fund our entire upper education in this country for five years or more.

There is no reason at all we couldn't have a 5% tax on all endowments and use the money to fund every one in this country that wants to go to college. It isn't going to affect these colleges in any way as they still have professional fundraisers traveling the country raising money as if they needed it.

Let's eliminate all the grants and loan programs and bureaucracy and use the endowment tax to fund college education to everyone free of charge.

Much has been said how we have a shortage of scientist and engineers in this country and nobody has come up with a viable solution to this problem.

Why not let capitalism take charge of the situation. A simple solution would be use the tax code to solve this problem. If we have a shortage of medical students or scientist or engineers in the country, put these graduates in a very low income tax bracket if they will work in these fields.

Make up for it by raising the tax rates on ambulance chasing lawyers and hedge fund managers to 90%. Money in a real capitalist society always manages to work itself out. Using the tax code as both a deterrent and an incentive can easily head our country in the direction we all would like to see.

Sense vs. Nonsense

This chapter will cover a wide array of topics which seem to have little if any thought or discussion about them. These topics include things that seem to go under the radar, so to speak, without notice.

First of all, since when does our space program, NASA have a blank check so to speak. Nobody ever talks about the billions spent on the space program every year or even consider whether that money would be better spent here in our own country. The only thing we should be sending to outer space at this time is about five hundred or so Washington politicians.

Why is it that the NASA can spend billions spying on everyday Americans phone and Internet conversations but can't spend that money to build the government their own secure Internet system?

As far as our military is concerned the American people need to come to the realization just how horrific war is and how wrong minded our military leaders have been for the last fifty years. It's not their fault they're just following the wishes of the American people who somehow came to the conclusion that it's just awful for military to kill our enemy's women and children. For over fifty years every conflict our military become involved in, the American people for some reason felt it is better to have our own soldiers killed, or physically, or mentally disabled for life, than to kill our enemy's women and children.

Until the American people truly realize how horrific war is, and not just a really good movie, the sooner they will realize its better to kill your enemy's women and children than let their soldiers kill and maim our own soldiers.

Only until you and they realize that their women and children are at risk will they ever truly fear you militarily speaking. Fear is a deterrent that cannot be equaled.

This isn't the 18th century anymore where the

soldiers line up in gentlemanly fashion and shoot at only other soldiers. WAR IS HELL!

About fifty years ago they took all the cigarette commercials off of television because of the health concerns. No mention has been made of all the ill effects alcohol has on our society. There are health concerns to an individual besides the alcoholism and the ill effects it has on our families.

At least cigarettes are basically a self inflicted vice that mostly hurts the user themselves. Of course, there's going to be some argument about second hand smoke, but the point is why are cigarette commercials banned and alcohol not. Either both should be allowed or both be banned. Why should one be singled out over the over?

Easily accessible pornography and gambling over the internet. Who in their right mind thinks this is a good thing? Unless you're in these industries of course.

Identity theft should be more of an impossibility

instead of a problem. You should never be allowed to get a credit card or a loan through the Internet or the mail. Those should be transactions that should be required to be done in person in a bank, reducing the possibility of identity theft entirely.

Today there are over a hundred channels on satellite and cable television and still nothing to watch. Because Congress passed a law that all of these channels get reimbursed for broadcasting their programming we are all stuck with exurbanite television bills and very poor programing.

If everyone could choose only the channels they want and pay for those, there would only be about forty channels left, at the most, and at a lesser cost to everyone and a better incentive for better programming as well.

Everyone should check out the financials of their publicly traded local utility. Most have huge amounts of debt and still pay out large amounts of cash dividends to shareholders on a quarterly basis. With a little investigation you will find you're paying between $20 and $30 or more per month to pay for these dividends. Wouldn't

It make more sense for these companies to forego the dividend and use the funds to retire their debt?

Every nonprofit tax free corporation including churches should be required to prepare quarterly financial statements that should be made available to anyone upon request. Most people don't realize there are now more nonprofit corporations in America than for profit ones. This is done mostly to avoid paying taxes.

Everyone that contributes to any nonprofit corporation should have access to their financial statements so they can make an informed decision on who they are giving money to and exactly what they are doing with it.

A gross revenue tax of 5% should be placed on all these so called nonprofit organizations and take the money to build mental hospitals or facilities to house the huge numbers of homeless people in this country that most suffer some sort of mental disorder.

Every dime or asset confiscated in every drug bust should be pooled and used entirely on drug treatment, rehabilitation, and drug prevention. A nationwide drug prevention plan can do more good to lesson the flow of drugs into this country by reducing their market in the first place.

Why is it that the FBI can raid someone's home and confiscate their computers because they are downloading child pornography, but they can't seem to catch those disgusting individuals that are putting it on the internet in the first place? Anyone distributing or filming child pornography should be given the death penalty.

Has it occurred to anyone that during recent

times, as well as the past, civil unrest situations that involved the police show that they haven't really changed their tactics in fifty years. Tear gas, water cannons, and dogs only seem to incite more hostility instead of calming it.

If they can send a man to the moon they should be able to develop a safe and dependable tranquilizer gun for police to use on rioters. After ten policeman shoot their third round of tranquilizer into a crowd of rioters there would be about thirty protesters down and out ready to go to jail. The rest would see that suddenly this isn't fun anymore and the odds of them being arrested went way up and off they'd go on their way home.

Conclusion

As a child, I saw two separate old black and white video clips on television that are forever etched into my mind.

First, was Dr. Martin Luther Kings I have a dream speech. Everyone has seen it at one time or another, I hope It's on the internet and viewing should be required by our children in school.

Another was a short clip from a speech Bobby Kennedy gave when he said "Some men see things as they are and say why, I see things as the way they could be and say why not?"

In closing although we may have lots of problems in this country we must realize that this is still the greatest country on earth, but as true Americans we are always striving for something better.

I have a dream that someday one of these common sense ideas will take root and make a significant difference in our society in the future. Why not?